KABOOM!

WHAT HAPPENS WHEN VOLCANOES ERUPT?

GEOLOGY FOR BEGINNERS

Children's Geology Books

n this book, we're going to talk about what happens when volcanoes erupt. So, let's get right to it!

When hot rock from under the Earth's surface erupts through an opening in the crust, a volcano is formed. The Earth's tectonic plates are in motion. They spread apart, crunch together, or slide beside or under one another. The fault lines located between these plates are where volcanoes form.

Activity at Mount Bromo in the early morning.

WHAT IS MAGMA AND WHAT IS LAVA?

The core of the Earth is partly made up of molten rock. When it's underground, it's called magma. When this molten rock erupts out of a volcano and spills out above ground, it's called lava. When it first comes out of a volcano, the temperature of lava is between 700 to 1,200 degrees Celsius, which is the same as 1,292 to 2,192 degrees Fahrenheit.

Eventually, lava that is flowing on the surface will stop moving and cool down. When it does, it creates igneous rocks such as basalt and obsidian.

Volcanoes are the way that the Earth emits its internal pressurized heat. Earth is not the only celestial body in our Solar System that has volcanoes. In fact, one of Jupiter's four largest moons is the most volcanically active body in our Solar System.

Volcano eruption.

On Earth, there are over 800 million people living in over 80 different countries who are within the range of 100 kilometers from a volcano. Large regions of the Philippines and Mexico as well as Japan, Ethiopia, and Indonesia are at risk. Indonesia, which is located on the volcanic region called the "ring of fire," is the most dangerous of these countries.

Volcano erupting lava, ashes, and smoke.

Two of the largest and deadliest volcanic eruptions that took place on Earth, the Tambora eruption in 1815, which killed over 60,000 people, and the Krakatau eruption in 1883, which killed over 34,000 people, were both in Indonesia.

About 74,000 years ago, the Toba eruption in Indonesia was one of the most powerfully destructive. It created a 100 kilometer by 60 kilometer caldera, which is now Lake Toba.

Active Volcano.

A caldera is crater that's formed by an eruption so strong that it collapses the volcano's mouth. When Toba erupted, it sent ash all the way to the Himalayan mountains located 3,000 kilometers northwest of it.

Geologists hope that by studying these past eruptions, they can find better methods for understanding and possibly predicting volcanic eruptions.

Volcano outburst.

Active Lava Flow at Twilight.

WHAT IS A VOLCANIC ERUPTION?

Suppose you have a bottle of soda. Soda has bubbles in it from carbonated gas. Before you take the bottle cap off you don't see too many bubbles. The bottle's pressure keeps the gas from bubbling. Instead, it stays dissolved in the soda.

However, if you open it, the pressure releases and the bubbles start to leave. If you shake it up before you open it, the soda will rush out explosively.

This is similar to the inner workings of a volcano. The liquid rock underground called magma is less dense than the heavier rocks around it.

Anak Krakatau volcano erupting with gray smoke.

Under intense heat and pressure, it will start to rise to the surface. As it moves toward the surface, bubbles from underground gases start churning.

These bubbles of gas start to exert a huge amount of pressure. The pressure drives the magma to the surface and sometimes forces it way up in the air before it spills out of the volcano.

Volcano Eruption.

W hen a volcanic eruption occurs, the volcano lets out clouds of ash, flowing lava, and sometimes volcanic bombs, which are huge lumps of lava that can be thrown far distances. Even though lava flows don't usually move very fast, they're very dangerous and so is the hot ash.

In the year 79 AD, Mount Vesuvius, located near the Bay of Naples, in Italy erupted sending hot ash over the city of Pompeii and burying alive anyone who had been foolish enough not to see the warning signs and get out of the area. At the beginning, the ash began to fall over the city, but there was still time to escape until a pyroclastic surge happened.

Poisonous gas at a superheated temperature and hot ash poured out of the volcano at a speed of 100 miles per hour and killed everything in its path. Over 2,000 people died.

A group of explorers found the site in 1748 and it was almost perfectly preserved under the thick layers of ash. Mount Vesuvius is still an active volcano.

THREE STAGES OF A VOLCANO

There are three distinct stages in the "life" of a volcano:

- Active, which is when a volcano is currently erupting or showing signs that it might erupt at any time.

- Dormant, which is when a volcano hasn't been active for a while, but could erupt again

- Extinct, which is when a volcano is not likely to erupt again

TYPES OF VOLCANOES

When we see pictures of volcanoes they are usually shown as tall mountains that are cone-shaped. However, there are actually four different types of shapes.

Krakatau erupts plume of smoke.

CINDER CONES

Cinder cone volcanoes are usually only 1,000 feet or less in height. They form from lava particles and blobs that are emitted from a single vent at the peak.

COMPOSITE VOLCANOES

These volcanoes are also cone-shaped, but they are formed from layers upon layers of lava that have been happening over hundreds if not thousands of years. The layers can continue to build until they are over 8,000 feet in height.

Lava lake of Erta Ale volcano, Ethiopia.

SHIELD VOLCANOES

Shield volcanoes have thin lava that spreads out wide. Eventually, the shape they form looks like a shield.

LAVA DOMES

When very thick lava gets hard around the outside of the vent it forms a lava dome. Sometimes this shape forms inside other volcano types.

Lava Ocean Entry.

Volcano eruption.

HOW DO VOLCANOES ERUPT?

All volcanoes have the same type of structure. Hot liquid magma forms a huge, bubbling cauldron under the volcano. A single vent starts forming from this magma chamber to the surface allowing magma to escape. Now that it's flowing out of the volcano, the hot molten rock is called lava. Secondary vents also form.

After an eruption blows the top right off the volcano, a crater is formed at the peak. Eruptions happen when intense pressure forces the magma from the chamber up through the main vent and secondary vents.

The mud that's created when the lava and ash mixes with rain or snow causes fast-moving mudslides that along with the hot lava can cause massive destruction.

Volcano eruption.

HOW DO VOLCANOES EXPLODE?

Different types of volcanoes explode in different ways. When volcanoes have thin lava sometimes it just slowly oozes out. When their lava is thick, it sometimes clogs up the volcano's vent. When this happens, pressure builds and builds. When it finally erupts, it does so with an enormous explosion. Lava and ash and volcanic bombs go everywhere.

Lava Ocean Entry, Kilauea, Hawaii.

VOLCANOES ARE
IMPORTANT TO
LIFE ON EARTH

According to the United States Geological Survey, despite their destructive power, volcanoes are critical to life on Earth. The gases released from volcanoes at the beginning of Earth's formation helped to create the atmosphere as well as the ocean. Over 80 percent of Earth's surface was formed one way or another through volcanic activity that produced plains as well as hills and mountains.

Deposits from volcanoes, such as basalt, are used to create important building materials. Volcanoes are still forming new islands on the surface of the Earth. Once the ash cools down it forms a nutrient rich habitat for plants.

Bárdarbunga volcanic eruption, Iceland.

Volcanic Eruption in Holuhraun Iceland.

FASCINATING FACTS ABOUT VOLCANOES

- A large eruption can level the entire area of a forest.

- At any given time, there are about 20 volcanic eruptions happening worldwide.

- Olympus Mons is the tallest volcano in our Solar System. It's a shield volcano on the Martian surface that is three times the height of Mount Everest. Scientists believe the last time it erupted was between 20 to 200 million years ago. They think it's extinct, but are not absolutely sure.

- A volcano on the Big Island of Hawaii is the largest one on Earth. It's called Mauna Loa and its last eruption was in 1984. The tallest volcano is Mauna Kea, which stands right next to Mauna Loa. Mauna Kea's last eruption was 4,000 to 6,000 years ago so it is considered to be dormant.

Lava lake.

- Volcanic ash is extremely harmful for people to breathe. It's also very dangerous for planes when it's in the atmosphere. In 2010, an active volcano in Iceland erupted and created a huge cloud of ash, which shut down Europe's airports for several days.

- Over a quarter of a million people have died from volcanic eruptions over the past 300 years.

- There are about 1,900 active volcanoes on our planet that have either erupted recently or might erupt. Over 80 volcanoes have been found submerged in the ocean.

- Most of the volcanoes are in the *"ring of fire,"* a large area in the Pacific Ocean.

Awesome! Now you know more about the science behind why volcanoes erupt. You can find more Geology books from Baby Professor by searching the website of your favorite book retailer.

Visit

BABY PROFESSOR
EDUCATION KIDS

www.BabyProfessorBooks.com

to download Free Baby Professor eBooks
and view our catalog of new and exciting
Children's Books